Stepparenting: Becoming A Stepparent

A Blended Family Guide To Parenting, Raising Children, Family Relationships and Step Families

By:
Mathew Massimo
and
Sofia Price

Matthew Massimo and Sofia Price

the trademark owner. All trademarks and brands within this book are for clarifying purposes only and are the owned by the owners themselves, not affiliated with this document.

Table of Contents

Matthew Massimo and Sofia Price

Introduction

I want to thank you and congratulate you for downloading the book, *"**Stepparenting: Becoming A Stepparent: A Blended Family Guide to: Parenting, Raising Children, Family Relationships and Step Families.**"*

This book contains proven steps and strategies on how to ease into your new role as a stepparent. Children are blessings from God. Whether they are yours biologically or by marriage, you can always strive to create a successful family in which everyone is committed to loving and caring for one another. It is possible to bring harmony to a blended or stepfamily. The road toward success may be more difficult than that for a new or nuclear family, but the rewards and joys you will gain are truly worth all the effort.

Parenting your own kids is challenging enough; parenting your stepchildren is even more difficult. Blended families that include you and your partner, your exes, your stepchildren, and your biological children face more issues and challenges than an average nuclear family. This is because there are more people involved, and the more people that are involved, the more complicated the relationships among the members will be.

It is a great challenge for stepparents to raise their partner's children because these kids are, in some way, affected by their other parent. You cannot and should not compete with their other parent, and you should love your stepchildren the way you love your own kids. You need to find the right balance between being a parent who imposes strict rules and a parent who can be their friend. You want your stepchildren to like you, but you also want them to respect you and treat you as a real parent.

This book gives you some useful tips and techniques on how to raise your stepchildren. It will give you an idea of how blended families can become successful. You will learn some tips on how to bond with your stepchildren, how you can deal with differences, how to strengthen your family as a whole, and how you can keep your relationship with your spouse happy so that the children will likewise feel safe and happy.

Thanks again for downloading this book. I hope you enjoy it!

Chapter 1 – Understanding Expectations in Blended Families

Before entering in a relationship with someone who has been married before and has kids, it is important that you understand the concept of having a blended family. A blended family includes not only you, your partner, and your kids, but also your children from your past relationships and your exes. It is definitely more complicated than a traditional nuclear family, but it can also be more rewarding when you know how to handle a blended family properly.

Being happy and comfortable in a blended family is not something that happens overnight. It requires more time and effort from the parents and the kids to make a blended family work. It is especially important for the parents to work extra hard to make their family work because it is not the kids' fault that they are in this situation. It is the parents' decision to split and remarry, and the kids should be spared of any pain and complications as much as possible. However, this does not mean that the kids should not do their own part because they also have to cooperate if they want to be happy and comfortable with their new family. It may take a long time and a lot of work from each person involved, but it will be worth it in the end.

You and your partner may be so excited to get married, and you likely have a lot of positive expectations about building a life together. However, you need to keep in mind that it is a different thing altogether with the kids. The kids have to make changes and adjustments in their lives because of YOUR decision. Many children whose parents separated also find it difficult to come to terms with one of their parents loving someone else other than their other parent. This makes it even more difficult for them to accept their stepparent.

Aside from this, children may also have to live with their stepsiblings, which can cause difficulties if you do not know how to manage a blended family the right way. Although some blended families have members who instantly like one another, there are those who do not want to have anything to do with their stepfamily. You should not give up easily because this is normal. What you can do is to carefully plan how your blended family will function even before you decide to get married to a partner who has kids from his or her past relationship. Here are some realistic expectations and the basic foundations of a blended family:

Children feel unsettled because of the many changes happening in their lives all at once. You need to consider this when thinking about starting a blended family. You need to take things slow for the sake of the kids. According to studies, couples who wait at least a couple of years after the divorce before getting remarried are more likely to have a successful family life. This is because the children were able to have plenty of time to adjust well after their parents split up before entering another kind of life in which they will have an additional parent and instant siblings.

It takes time to really love your stepchildren the way you love your own kids, the same way that it takes time for your stepchildren to love you the way they love their biological parent. You need to give plenty of time for your relationship to blossom naturally by spending time together and getting to know one another well. Remember that love and affection does not happen overnight.

You should spend time with your stepchildren and biological children to experience normal day-to-day life with them. It is fun to take them out to theme parks and special places from time to time, but it is important for you to experience "real life" with them. After all, you do not go to Disneyland or the zoo every day. You stay in your house most of the time and do ordinary things. You and your stepchildren have to get used to the normal routine that you have at home.

Before marrying someone who already has children, it is important that he or she makes the necessary parenting changes. This way, the kids will not resent you for the unexpected and sudden changes in their lives. You need to talk to your partner about the kinds of house rules that you want to impose when you are married. For instance, before you enter their lives, your partner should impose the curfew that you have talked about that is earlier than what they are used to. By doing this, they will not think that you are the villain in your household by having to impose stricter rules.

You should also avoid giving ultimatums or making your spouse choose between you and the stepchildren. Your stepchildren will only dislike you more because it is as if you are trying to take away their other parent from them.

You cannot force your stepchildren to love you right away, but you should definitely insist on respect. They may not like you, but it is important that they respect you. As a stepparent, you should also show respect to your stepchildren.

You need to avoid setting high expectations. As previously mentioned, it takes time to build love and affection in your relationship. You should not expect that everyone will get along with one another right away because you will only feel disappointed. Do not give up immediately because your relationship will surely work out in the end if you do things properly.

With the right kind of love and support toward your stepchildren, they will slowly adjust to being a member of a new family. Given that you are the parent, it is your obligation to ensure that the kids make a smooth transition from one kind of family to another.

Matthew Massimo and Sofia Price

Chapter 2 – Prioritize your Marriage

It is possible to have a solid marriage and a loving family life with your stepchildren. However, you should understand and realize that before you can have a successful stepfamily, you need to become a successful step couple first. The stability and happiness of the whole family will rely on the quality and strength of your relationship with your husband or wife.

You may prepare yourself before getting into a stepfamily, but there will always be challenges that you can never fully prepare for. This is the reason why your relationship with your spouse needs to be solid and strong, and keeping your marriage healthy and stable is something that you need to continuously work on. Here are the four core skills that you should focus on:

- Nurture the love connection between you and your spouse

- Learn how to communicate effectively

- Become creative co-parents

- Strive to clarify unsettled issues you might have from your previous marriages or relationships

Stepfamilies are unlike nuclear families in different fundamental ways. A complete nuclear family begins with a marriage, and the kids are then added to the mix. In a blended family, the kids are present right at the start and even before the marriage. Because of this, blended families are more dynamic than nuclear families.

It is critical that your relationship with your spouse becomes a top priority, particularly more important than that with your kids, because the foundation of a strong family is built on a strong marriage, not around the kids. You need to commit to a lifetime of working on your marriage, continuing to pursue each other, and meeting each other's needs. This truth is actually applicable to both nuclear and blended families.

However, this is not to say that you should disregard your kids. Your children are also very important elements of your family, but they are not as essential as your marriage. If you choose to prioritize your children at the expense of your marriage, the latter will suffer, which can ultimately make your children suffer as well. In many instances, parents of a blended family have undergone divorce from a previous relationship, which means that the kids have already experienced an unsuccessful marriage. This makes your part as their role model more important because they need to see that a successful marriage is possible.

Raising your children is a temporary task in your life. When they have grown, they will eventually leave your home to start their own lives, but your marriage will last for the rest of your life, long after the kids have left your nest and even after your friends have come and gone. If you neglect your marriage for the sake of your kids, you will be setting yourself up for pain and heartache later in life. Such neglect will cause you to be left with an empty shell of a marriage after your kids have grown up.

What is worse is that your kids will not have a flourishing marriage to emulate when they enter marriage themselves. Anything that you do with your marriage now could carry on for several generations. If your marriage is successful, then you are also increasing the chances of your children having successful marriages.

Chapter 3 – Know your Role as a Stepparent

No one can argue that becoming a stepparent is truly one of the hardest roles you can ever take on as an adult. You will be able to avoid a lot of pain and hurt if you and your spouse agree at the onset on a few basic definitions of your role as a stepparent. This will enable you to be aware of the sensitivities that come with the role.

You and your spouse need to spend enough time to discuss openly and candidly any expectations and fears that you might have about your role as a stepparent. It will really make your role a lot easier when both you and your spouse know how you plan to guide, supervise, and discipline your stepchildren. After you have understood both of your roles, you can then proceed to define how you want to proceed with your role as a stepparent. You can begin by identifying the things that both of you can agree on. This can aid in narrowing your differences.

How you want your role as a stepparent to be is definitely up to you. However, you can use the following suggestions to see what you think will work for you and your family:

- It is a lot easier for you to ease into the role of a stepparent when you were brought into the blended family when the kids were still very young. You would have easily gained the role of the mother or father to your stepchildren and, as such, you will not find it too hard to discipline them. I know that each blended family is different but, in most instances, it is a lot harder to discipline stepchildren because you can create resentment from your spouse's end.

  If your spouse is understanding and does not take it against you when you discipline his or her kids, I am happy for you because that means you have an extra resource in handling discipline issues with your stepchildren. As a stepparent, you are not likely to be very effective as a direct disciplinarian to your stepchildren. However, you need to realize that you still need to be an active supporter of your spouse's efforts when it comes to disciplining the children. You and your spouse should agree on which house rules you will implement and the standards that you will hold the children to.

- Although you will not be actively initiating any direct discipline relative to your stepchildren, you still need to work on maintaining the boundaries that should naturally exist between you and them. Even though your spouse serves the initial consequences for misbehavior, you need to show your active support of his/her decisions. You and your spouse should also ensure that you are given the appropriate respect and acknowledgement. This means that a stepmother should not be viewed by the stepchildren as merely their father's wife. She is actually an adult and authority figure inside the home.

- When you relate to all the kids – both biological and stepchildren – you need to define your relationship with them as both their supporter and ally. Whether you are the same or opposite-sexed parent, your presence can definitely help in balancing your role as a model and an information-giver about life from your own perspective. However, you should never misconstrue your role as supporter and ally as a replacement for their true biological mother or father.

- You also need to avoid having unrealistic expectations about your level of intimacy or closeness with your stepkids. Keep in mind that you need to build your relationships with them, and it could take a lot of time and many shared experiences before you can have a meaningful relationship with your stepchildren. You also need to be mindful of that fact that your stepchildren may also be going through their own share of emotional confusion. They may be feeling guilty that they are letting down their own biological father or mother when they start feeling close to you. It is crucial to practice utmost care and patience while you are allowing your stepchildren to work through their emotions.

- You need to actively support the relationship of your stepchildren with their own biological father or mother, who is not part of your home. If you are taking on the role of a stepmother, then you need to prioritize nurturing a relationship between you and your stepchildren's biological mother. You should look for all possible ways to support the relationship between your stepchildren and their mother. This may seem like taking the high road. However, if you do this, you will discover that it will be easier for you to remove any feelings of resentment from both your stepchildren and their biological mother.

  You need to know that this will necessitate real commitment from your end because when you support the relationship of your stepchildren with their biological parent, it could appear that you are also supporting the relationship of your spouse with his or her ex-spouse. You should not allow envy or jealousy to get the best of you. Be secure in your spouse's love and commitment to you so that you can allow him or her to have a working relationship with the ex-spouse.

- If your family is a truly blended one in which you and your spouse both have children from previous relationships, you should be careful not to appear to have favorites. Do not have double standards, with your own children receiving special treatment over your stepkids. It is natural for you to have stronger connections with your own biological kids, but this normally happens only while starting your new family.

For you to establish real harmony at home, you need to avoid showing any differences in how you treat your own biological kids and your stepchildren. As you gain more shared life experiences with both your biological children and stepchildren, you will realize that your connection and affection for all children will start to become equal. It is ideal if you can measure and balance the actual time you spend on all your children, both biological and non-biological, including the activities and money you spend on them.

Chapter 4 – Know Your Stepchildren's Needs

You already know the basic needs children have, such as food, clothing, shelter, and education. These things are not difficult to know and to provide as long as you have the money. Aside from these things, kids also have another set of needs that are more emotional rather than physical or mental. If you want to establish a good relationship between you and your stepchildren, you need to focus on providing their needs. These are basic emotional needs that every human being should have. If the kids can see or feel that you are making an effort to provide them what they need, they will like you more, and your relationship with them will be so much easier. The age or gender of the child does not matter because these are the basic emotional needs of every individual.

Your stepchildren want to feel:

- **Loved.** Everyone wants to feel loved. You should show love and affection toward your stepchildren if you want them to show you the same thing. You should always make decisions based on your love for them. Just keep in mind that reciprocating this love may take time. Also, you should not force yourself to love your stepchildren immediately because it will show. Just let your love for one another develop gradually. You can also show your love by imposing reasonable limits and boundaries. They may show that they do not like it, but they prefer that you set limits and boundaries because it makes them feel worthy and cared for. Just remember to talk about it with your spouse before imposing rules.

- **Safe and secure.** When their parents get a divorce and remarry, kids feel unsecure because they know what kinds of changes they will have in their lives and what adjustments they will need to make once their parents remarry. It is important to give them normalcy and stability to make them feel safe and secure. You should also make an effort to make them trust you as their parent.

- **Heard.** You need to have an open line of communication if you want to make your stepchildren feel heard. When they talk, you should listen and understand what they are saying. You may be older, but this does not mean that you should be the only one talking. When you listen to what they are saying, they will feel emotionally connected to you as their new parent. By listening, you are showing them that you want to understand where they are coming from and that you want to empathize with them.

- **Valued.** To show your stepchildren that you value them, you should include them when making decisions, especially those that will affect their lives. Children rarely get involved in the decision-making process, and they will feel valued when you consult them or ask their opinion when making important decisions.

- **Appreciated.** When your stepchildren accomplish something, you should appreciate their effort. You should also appreciate the things that they do in the house to make your relationship with them work. You can simply say "thank you" or treat them to a dinner or a trip to an amusement park to show them that you appreciate their efforts and accomplishments.

- **Encouraged.** When your stepchildren want to pursue something, like a hobby or passion, you need to show them encouragement. For instance, if your stepchild loves to play the piano, you can enroll him or her in a piano class or buy a baby piano. You should also show them encouragement in their schoolwork, especially if they are struggling with a specific subject. Showing encouragement is like telling them that you believe in their ability and that they can achieve what they want as long as they put their minds to it.

- **Respected.** They may be younger than you, but you should respect your stepchildren the way you want to be respected. For instance, you should listen to what they have to say when talking to them. You should also respect their privacy by not meddling in their private lives or not entering their room without knocking. If you give them the respect that they want, they will find it easier to respect you as a parent as well. This is one of those aspects of life that go both ways.

These are the emotional needs of your stepchildren that you need to meet as a stepparent. It is important that you allow the kids to set their own pace when it comes to you getting to know them. You should not force yourself on them or force them to do things with you because this will only make them dislike you. You should also consider the kids' personalities. For example, you need to slow down your pace when dealing with shy, introverted kids. Give them plenty of time to open up to you. They will warm up to you when they feel comfortable enough. To make them warm up to you, just show them that you are interested in their lives, but do not invade their privacy. You can show interest in their lives by asking questions about their day, attending their school activities, listening to their stories, and encouraging them to pursue their passion and hobbies. Do not force them to tell you anything because they will tell you when they are ready.

If the other parent has passed away and you are marrying the other parent, you need to give plenty of time and space for the children to grieve. In fact, it is best not to get married at least a couple of years after the death of their parent. Otherwise, they will just resent you, especially if they were close with their deceased parent. They need to be able to grieve for their parent completely before they can move on and start a new life with a new family because it is difficult to deal with someone who is still in pain.

Matthew Massimo and Sofia Price

Chapter 5 – Learn How Kids Adjust to Blended Families

Different kids have different ways of coping and adjusting to changes in their life, like their parents remarrying and having a stepparent and stepsiblings. Some are able to adjust easily without a problem, whereas others have more trouble adjusting. You need to exert extra effort if the child finds it difficult to adjust. The way they cope and adjust to changes in their life depends on several factors like age, personality, and gender. For example, toddlers have different coping skills compared with teenagers; the same thing goes for boys versus girls. You need to choose the right approach based on these factors. Just remember that your ultimate goal is for them to accept and love you as one of their parents.

Here is a guide that will let you know how different children adjust to being a part of a blended family.

Children aged 10 years and below

Younger children adjust more easily than older children because they still have a very limited knowledge of the situation. They are more willing to accept a new adult in their life, especially if the adult treats them nicely. Getting them to like you is something as simple as giving them a toy or playing with them. Just make sure that you do not give them material things all the time because you do not want them to like you for the wrong reasons. You should also show them your love by doing other things, such as helping them with their homework or taking care of them when they are sick. They also feel competitive for their parent's attention, so be sure to allow your partner who is their real parent to spend more time with their kids so that your stepchildren will not feel that you are trying to take their parent away from them. Younger kids also have more daily needs because they are still dependent on an adult's help. For instance, you still need to prepare their food or choose clothes for them. If you are able to provide them with their daily needs, these young kids will be more likely to accept you as their stepparent because you act just like their real parent.

Adolescents aged 10 to 14

Adolescents will probably have the most difficult time adjusting to a blended family. This is because these children are still finding their own identity and are experiencing a lot of changes in their life, both physical and emotional. Being forced into a situation that they did not choose will only make things more difficult for them. They have to make certain adjustments once they are a member of a blended family on top of the adjustments that they need to make because of the changes happening in their life. They require more time to accept a new adult in their life, especially someone who will be a parent-figure. It is more difficult for them to accept the new rules that you have made, so be sure to talk to your partner before making any changes in house rules. They may not say it, but they also need love and attention. They have a difficult time expressing their feelings, so you have to be sensitive and learn how to read gestures and actions.

Teenagers aged 15 and older

Stepchildren aged 15 and older tend to separate themselves from their family and prefer to be with their friends. They also start to form their own identities and their own lives outside their home. They are busy with school or work, which divides their attention between their family life and life outside their home. They are less involved with their family life, which makes them more accepting of having a stepparent. Teenagers aged 15 and older also tend to express themselves better than younger teens, which makes it easier for you to understand their needs and wants.

Boys versus girls

When it comes to adjusting to blended families, boys and girls show both similarities and differences. One similarity is that both genders prefer verbal affection over physical closeness. They prefer compliments or praises over hugs and kisses. Step daughters tend to feel awkward around their stepfathers, especially when it comes to displaying physical affection. Needless to say, boys become comfortable more quickly around their stepfathers than girls.

Matthew Massimo and Sofia Price

Chapter 6 – How to Handle Differences in a Blended Family

Larger families tend to have more differences, which makes it more difficult for them to get along with one another. It becomes even more difficult if it is a blended family because the members come from different families with different backgrounds and house rules. Major changes and adjustments are necessary to make the family members get along with one another, especially the stepparents and stepchildren.

Merging two families is not an easy thing to do because of differences in lifestyle, parenting, discipline, house rules, and so on. It is important to have consistency in discipline, chores, rules, and allowances to avoid jealousy and resentment. You and your spouse should always show that you are united when it comes to house rules and other family issues. This will avoid any feelings of resentment and unfairness.

Understanding the differences within blended families will make it easier for you and your children to adjust to your new family structure and life in general. Here are some common differences that you need to consider when starting a blended family:

Differences in age

If you have your own children and your partner also has children from his or her past relationship, there will surely be age differences among the children. It can be more difficult if the kids are all adolescents, who are more emotionally sensitive and may tend to feel more jealous and insecure. It may be easier if the kids are all young because they can treat one another as playmates. Of course, it still depends on the situation and how kids are brought up and their different personalities. It is also possible that one parent is just a few years older than the eldest stepchild, which can be especially awkward. It is also possible that the stepparent is younger than the eldest child. These differences in age should be considered when starting a blended family because it will affect how you should interact with and treat one another. For instance, if the eldest child is an adult who is older than the stepparent, the stepparent should not meddle with the stepchild's life and should not impose rules and discipline. The stepparent may be viewed as an equal rather than as a parent.

Differences in roles

When parents remarry, the children may need to adjust to changes in roles. For instance, one child may be the oldest in his original family, but after his parent remarries, he may find himself as one of the youngest among the children. He may be an only child, but he may suddenly have instant siblings once one of his parents remarries. It can also mean losing one's uniqueness by no longer being the only boy or only girl among his or her siblings. These changes can affect the child's behavior and acceptance of the new blended family, so be sure to take note of this.

Differences in parenting style

One parent may not have any previous experience raising kids, and this can affect his or her parenting style. The other parent should guide his or her partner and should understand that there will be shortcomings because of inexperience. Besides, the stepparent who never had kids before was not able to experience the different stages of child development. He or she was given instant children without experiencing raising the child from birth and seeing the different stages of childhood.

Other parenting differences involve house rules, discipline, allowances, and so on. This should be discussed before deciding to merge two families together so that the kids will not be confused and will not feel like they are being pulled in two different directions.

Differences in family traditions

Families have different ways of spending special holidays, birthdays, and vacations. Kids may feel resentful if there are changes in the traditions and routines that they are used to. For example, if they always go on a vacation abroad every Christmas but your new family cannot afford to do so, you can find a common ground like going on an out of town trip, or you can create a new and exciting tradition for your new blended family. Do not make any abrupt changes, especially in things that the kids love to do, because they will only dislike you as a stepparent. However, you should also not force yourself to follow their traditions if you cannot afford it just to please the kids. It is important to meet in the middle and make compromises by sitting down, talking it out, and consulting one another when making major changes and decisions that involve the whole family.

Differences in personality

There will surely be differences in personality among family members. For example, your biological kids may be outgoing and talkative, whereas your stepchildren may be shy and quiet. You need to know how to handle them based on their personality differences. Do not force shy children to be more outgoing because this will only make them feel resentful. Just let them set their own pace, especially when it comes to making friends in your new neighborhood or in their new school. As a parent, it is your responsibility to know your children and their personality so that you can find better and more effective parenting strategies for each of them.

Matthew Massimo and Sofia Price

Chapter 7 – How to Create your New Family Identity

It is part of human nature to seek a family in which we belong. Family rituals and traditions, anecdotes, and stories are important tools you can use in creating a unique identity for your family. This identity can give your stepchildren a sense of belonging because they share the same values, history, and even sense of humor with people they love and truly care for. Through your family identity, you and your spouse can pass on your family's history to all of your kids, which they can then learn from while carving out their own place in this world.

The most obvious way to build a family identity is by talking to your kids. This may seem simple, but it can be difficult, especially when you want to really talk to your kids. You can start by talking about your own life, how you were while growing up, and what their grandparents were like. However, why do many parents find it hard to talk to their kids about these simple facts? One reason is that they are not able to spend enough quality time with their kids. They are so used to transporting their children from one activity to the next, eagerly feeding them with fast food, and then dispatching them at night with a mere, "Don't forget to brush your teeth." Instead of talking to them during car drives, many parents opt to just listen to the radio while they let their kids play video games.

For you to be able to create your new family identity and to fortify your family tree for future generations, it is necessary that you create family rituals and traditions. Holiday traditions will be discussed in the next chapter. However, I want to emphasize here that the "regular" or usual traditions that your family does on a day-to-day basis are more important than the holiday traditions. Christmas, Thanksgiving, birthdays, and anniversaries only happen once a year. By contrast, our lives are mostly composed of regular days. Therefore, the traditions that you have on those regular days will have the biggest effects on your children.

These regular traditions can be as simple as reading a short story or a poem together on the living room couch after dinner, enjoying hot chocolate with marshmallows together on a cold or rainy day, or even kissing each other good night before sleeping. In just half an hour every night, you can have great effects on your stepchildren's lives by tucking them in with bedtime stories, having private talks, and saying prayers together. These simple acts can intensify your stepchildren's sense of belonging.

You can further enhance the relationships within your stepfamily, and thereby create a stronger family identity, by working as a team on different projects like gardening, creating homemade gifts, and even volunteering as a group at the local community shelter.

You can reinforce the feeling of trust and openness through simple statements you can utter anytime of the day like, "I feel so blessed to be part of a family who can talk about just everything!" or "I am so happy to be feeling this close to you." When you correct your step kids, you can tell them in a tender voice that, "Our family does not say 'shut up' to one another," "We do not drink straight from the milk carton," or "Our family likes to be helpful, kind, and polite to other people."

Camping is another family activity that is very effective in making families more bonded. When you are out in nature, you will be able to rely more on one another and be comforted that each member of the family is out there for support. Sitting around the bonfire at night is a good time to share stories that each one of you can treasure for the rest of your lives.

There are other ways for you to build the identity of your blended family and impart that identity to your stepchildren. You just need to be prepared to be more creative when thinking of activities that will be interesting for all members of the family and that will fit all your schedules. After you have decided on those activities, make sure that you make them a central part of everyone's lives. Just always keep in mind that your family identity can improve the lives of your stepchildren, and it can strengthen the foundation of your whole family.

Chapter 8 – Strengthen Your Blended Family

To be able to improve your relationship with your stepchildren, you need to find ways to strengthen your blended family as a whole. You can do this by creating trust between the parents and the children. The kids may feel uncomfortable and uncertain about their stepfamily and may pretend not to like your effort to be closer to them, but you still need to try. Do not easily give up or lose your patience when they do not show any enthusiasm or when they show a negative attitude toward all your efforts to get to know them better. They may show that they do not care or that they dislike your efforts, but deep down, they are happy that you show them that you care and that you love them even if you are not their real parent. Always remind yourself that any negative reactions from the stepchildren, especially for the first few months, are normal.

To strengthen your blended family, you need to do the following:

Set clear boundaries

To create trust in your blended family, you need to establish discipline within the household. Kids may resent you at first, but it is something that they will thank you for as time goes by. They will trust you as a parent because they know that you want to keep them safe and secure by imposing rules and discipline. It is important for couples to discuss their roles when it comes to taking disciplinary actions in raising their children.

To make the transition from one household to another, the stepparent should first serve as a counselor or a friend and the biological parent as the disciplinarian. This way, the child will not harbor any negative feelings toward his or her stepparent and will instead view his or her stepparent as a friend. Just let the biological parent handle disciplinary actions for his or her own children. The stepparent should not meddle until he or she has formed a solid bond with the children. You should discuss the new family rules with all the family members, especially the kids, so that everyone knows what is expected of them. You can write the rules and post them somewhere that can be easily seen, like the refrigerator door or family bulletin board. You need to take into consideration the differences among the kids, such as age and interests, when creating these rules. You should also understand the rules that the kids have to follow and the disciplinary actions while trying to be as consistent as possible.

Talk to ALL the parents

It is best to include the ex-spouse or your stepchildren's other biological parent to make it easier for the kids. If the kids know that the adults are trying their best to set aside their differences and work together for the sake of their children, the kids will feel more loved and appreciated and will consequently be more willing to accept their new blended family. It is important that the kids know that no matter what happens, their biological parents and the stepparents will be there for them and will continue to love them. Tell them that you are not going to replace their real mom or dad, but you are there as an additional parent, which means that there are more people to love and care for them.

Establish open and regular communication

Another way to build trust is to establish open and regular communication, especially with your stepchildren. Misunderstandings and confusion that can lead to fights and conflicts can be avoided if there is open and frequent communication. Poor communication often leads to unnecessary worries and uncertainties that can affect the relationships among family members. To establish good communication, you need to be a good listener, especially because you are their parent.

Whenever your stepchild has something to say, always listen respectfully. This way, your stepchild will do the same thing when you talk. Do not dismiss what your stepchild has to say just because he or she is still young. You need to listen to them, even the small ones, so that you can better understand their needs.

When discussing conflicts, it is important to do it in a positive way rather than finding fault or blaming someone. This is why establishing a nonjudgmental atmosphere in your household whenever there is a family discussion over a problem is highly encouraged. You should also schedule activities like sports and games that you can do with your stepchildren. This way, you have something to bond over that will make you feel more comfortable with one another and will make communication a lot easier.

Develop rituals and routines

In a family, routines and rituals keep the members united. This is especially helpful in a blended family. You should develop your own special routines and rituals, like movie night every Saturday, going to an out of town trip on birthdays, eating out once a month, and so on. By developing rituals and routines, you are providing the consistency and stability that your stepchildren and biological children need. This also allows you to create special moments and memories with your stepchildren that you can look back on when things are calmer and relationships are stronger.

Matthew Massimo and Sofia Price

Chapter 9 – How to Combine Holidays and Family Traditions

Almost all families have rituals or traditions. These pertain to the activities and patterns of interaction that families have on a day-to-day, weekly, monthly, and yearly basis. Greeting your family with a kiss and a hug when you get home is a ritual that is as important as the decades-old tradition of celebrating Thanksgiving at Grandmother's home. Traditions are essential elements of a family. They convey the identity of the family as a whole, and they offer security to different family members. Have you felt like a part of you died when one of your traditions was broken or altered? A lot of people do not realize the importance of traditions in their lives until they are no longer able to do them.

The belongingness and identity of your family are greatly connected to your traditions. During the first five to seven years of the family (also referred to as the integration years), you may observe that a positioning occurs between the insider and outsider members of the family, as each individual tries to keep his or her own traditions alive. The insiders are the members who are related to one another by blood, whereas the outsiders are the members who were blended to the family because of the new marriage. Anyone who does not share a particular tradition is made to feel like he or she is an outsider. This leads to a division in the family identity.

However, this is actually a natural phenomenon, especially because the blended family has not yet been given sufficient time to bring harmony in the group. For you to find common ground for the traditions of the insiders and outsiders, everyone, especially the adults, should show a willingness to be flexible. The battle lines between the insiders and outsiders are normally drawn when the adults refuse to be accommodating to new changes.

Holiday traditions are particularly difficult to deal with during the early part of the blended family. It can be a lot worse when you and your ex-spouse are not on good terms; but even if you and your ex-spouse have a civil agreement regarding your kids, you cannot really stop your children from feeling certain sadness because they cannot be with both their biological parents and because they miss the traditions from their previous holidays. They may feel certain awkwardness while adjusting to new traditions, new food, and even new people.

Below are some practical techniques you can use in merging your holiday and family rituals and traditions.

• Be flexible, and be willing to make some sacrifices. It is quite impossible to make everybody happy all the time. When you understand this truth, you will no longer be pressured to provide everyone with what they want. Becoming flexible means that you are willing to merge, alter, or even sacrifice your old traditions during a particular year so that you can give your new stepfamily a chance to create new traditions. You can show your stepchildren that you are willing to negotiate and to sacrifice.

• Give importance to planning. You and your spouse should spend enough time planning your activities for upcoming holidays. This will allow both of you to share your preferences, desires, and any required sacrifices that you are willing to make for the benefit of your whole family. After you and your spouse have planned, you can then contact your ex-spouses to begin negotiating. If you and your spouse both have ex-spouses, it is ideal to begin your holiday plans at an earlier time.

• Use your creativity. It is so easy to become busy with a lot of different things during the hectic holiday season. This is especially true when you and your spouse both have children from previous relationships. Because of this, you need to be more creative while you are integrating your old traditions and rituals to create new ones for your new stepfamily.

- Change what you can, and accept what you cannot change. It is important that you continue working on your marriage all throughout the year so that you can have a stronger and better relationship by the time the holidays come. Your marriage is one thing that you can change and improve, but one of the things that you need to accept as something you cannot fully control is your ex-spouse. Do not feel too frustrated when you do not always get what you want, and just place your frustrations at God's feet and move on.

- Be compassionate when it comes to your stepchildren's preferences during the holiday season. While teaching them to cooperate in the negotiation process, you need to be gentle and show compassion. Truly listen to what they have to say, and gently work through your differences.

Your day-to-day connection rituals are essential in integrating your family traditions. The small and simple things that your family does on a day-to-day basis to show your commitment, care, and concern are very important. Hugging your stepchildren before they leave for school or leaving special notes in their lunch boxes may seem simple, but they have lasting effects. Movie marathons and pizza on Friday nights are not only fun activities, but they can also help your whole family in starting new traditions.

Matthew Massimo and Sofia Price

Chapter 10 – Decide on Living Arrangements

When you create your stepfamily after marrying someone who has children from a previous relationship, one of the priority decisions you need to make is about the living arrangements of your stepchildren. You and your spouse, together with your spouse's ex, need to decide on which parent the kids should live with. You need to make sure that the preferences of not only the parents and stepparents, but also that of the children, are taken into consideration when making this major decision.

Here is the basic rule you need to follow when making this decision: kids must have constant contact with both their biological parents while growing up. They need to be reassured that their mother and father love them, even if they cannot be together as husband and wife anymore. They need to be reassured that even if their old family is no longer together, their parents will always be there for them. Your children will flourish when they feel loved, accepted, and approved of. Do not let them feel that they have been abandoned, because this may lead them to feel rejected and alone.

There are different kinds of living arrangements you can agree on for your stepchildren. Here are just some of them:

- Day visits or seeing the biological parent (not living with the children) for the day is ideal for kids who are still very young or when the biological parent who is not living with the kids (non-resident parent) does not live in a house where the kids can stay.

One of the advantages of this alternative is that very young children will not have to be frightened to stay overnight in another home, which could separate them from their regular routines. There are cases in which brief but regular contact is more advantageous than longer visits. If possible, invite the non-resident parent over to visit the house to make the children more comfortable.

Another advantage of day visits is that your stepchildren will have a chance to be with their non-resident parent, even if your spouse and his or her ex-spouse have not yet reached an agreement regarding the living arrangements. If the visits are difficult, you can hold them at a Child Contact Center, where you can drop off your stepchildren and collect them safely afterwards without having to face the ex-spouse.

One of the disadvantages of day visits is that older kids may see them as a threat. They may also fail to have the chance to be involved in the daily life of their non-resident parent, including his or her new family or new partner.

Both the parents and the kids may also take the day visits less seriously, which could lead to reduced commitment to keeping the arrangements as compared with longer stays. One or more of the involved parties may be tempted to cancel one visit when they think it will interfere with their plans. This cancelled visit will eventually become more frequent. In the end, your stepchildren may lose contact with their non-resident parent.

- Weekend visits, including school holidays, is the most common arrangement used by divorced or separated parents. One of the advantages of this arrangement is its simplicity. Your stepchildren can keep their own homes and own rooms. This continuity is actually very important for kids because it lets them maintain a support network from their friends, neighbors, and even their school. The breakup of their parents is hard enough, and this could become harder when your stepchildren will need to break up with their old support network.

One of the disadvantages of this setup is that the resident partner and his or her new family will not be able to spend quality time with the kids during weekends and school holidays. They will only be able to be with the kids during weekdays, which is when everyone needs to go to school and to work. Occasional visits can also place undue pressure on the kids because these can constantly remind them that their stay with both their resident and non-resident parents is temporary. They always need to be separated from either one of them.

They may start to feel that their lives are out of their control, particularly when they have to forgo a special event, such as a sleepover, a school event, or a birthday party of a friend, because they need to be at another house. They may face guilt and strained emotions as a result.

- Weekend visits plus holidays and one extra day each week is an arrangement that is ideal if you and your spouse live near the house of the ex-spouse. One of the advantages of this setup is that your stepchildren will have more contact with both their resident and non-resident parents. This will enable them to create deeper relationships with both of parents.

When the kids have one extra day during the middle of the week plus the weekends, they will have a better sense of being settled or "at home." In addition, the extended contact will enable both parents and stepparents to create a regular routine for the whole family, including the children, instead of merely leisure time during holidays and weekends.

One of the disadvantages of this alternative is that the extra night spent by the kids away from their primary home can disrupt their routine and bring more stress. This may leave them feeling confused, such that they may start having difficulties at home and at school. Either they keep two separate sets of clothes and supplies in both homes or they need to be utterly organized to ensure that everything they need is available when they need it.

All of you will need to have a clue as to where the children are and how they will stay connected with their families and friends. If you and the family of the ex-spouse have varying house rules and parenting styles, your children may end up confused and demoralized as well.

- The children spend equal time with their two parents. This can be done either one week for each parent or in three- or four-day blocks for each. Both the biological mother and biological father will enjoy equal amounts of time with their children. One of the advantages of this setup is that the two families will be able to spend longer periods of time with the children, both during weekdays and weekends. They will have an opportunity to build relationships with the kids. The children will be able to experience the normal lifestyle of having both parents, including following set house rules and regular routines.

The children will also have the opportunity to develop their own networks of friends at both homes, and those friends will be able to understand that the children actually have two homes. The children will also have better opportunities to negotiate with both parents when they want to go certain social events. This is particularly difficult with the first two alternatives.

The disadvantages of this alternative include the stress that both parents can undergo being away from their children for long periods of time. The kids, who may be distressed after they feel comfortable with one family only to have to transfer to the other family for a couple of days, can also experience this. They may find it harder to organize their social events because they always need to consider which home base they will be in.

How to decide on the best alternative for your children

You and the other parents and stepparents of the kids may wrongly assume that the final decision is for you to make, and the parent "left holding the baby" may think that they have the majority vote. In a lot of instances, the primary care of young kids is given to the mother. However, this may not always be the best option for kids, especially if this is not what they truly want.

Often, parents decide on the living arrangement of their kids based on their own reasoning, but this does not really involve just the kids, but the parents' welfare, as well. It is so common to see separated parents fighting for sole custody of the kids. This is especially common when one or both parents already have new partners or families.

There are even instances in which one of the partners stops the kids from contacting the other parent as a means of getting back at or punishing the ex-spouse. Sometimes, the reasoning used by parents for insisting that the children stay with them and have limited visits with the ex-spouse may really be rooted in their own negative feelings, such as pain, loss, rejection, and anger. Do not let these negativities cloud your judgment on what is truly beneficial for the kids.

When deciding about their living arrangements, it is always ideal for the kids to have a say, too. If the children are too young to speak for themselves or you think that they may be influenced by their need to please a certain parent, you can speak for them, but you need to put yourself in their shoes. Here are some points that you can consider when making a decision:

- Keep in mind your goal of having a lasting, loving, and successful relationship with the kids and the rest of your new blended family.

- You need to consider facilitating closure on the past relationship with the ex-partner so that all of you can start moving on from being ex-partners to being co-parents.

- Your spouse needs to reiterate his or her love and commitment to you.

- You need to consider how your stepchildren can be easily accessible, even when they are staying with the other biological parent.

- You need to consider the children's need to be able to easily access both of their biological parents.

- You also need to consider how your stepchildren and you and your own children can have enough time to create good relationships.

- You need to take into account the social needs of your children and ensure that they can nurture friendships and relationships with other family members, such as grandparents, aunts, uncles, and cousins.

- You need to consider the children's school requirements.

Around 50 percent of fathers start losing touch with their kids within two years of separation from the ex-spouse. Only a handful of those dads are really "deadbeat" and do not care; many of them are actually stunned by the hardships and pain that come with keeping contact with the kids. One of the reasons why second marriages have higher chances of splitting up than first marriages is the strain or stress that comes with dealing with the needs and emotions of everyone involved.

The best that you can really do to increase your chances of success is not to attempt to win the war. Learn how to negotiate until you reach an agreement that can satisfy everyone involved, including the children and the adults.

Chapter 11 – Do's and Don'ts of Step Parenting

To sum up everything that you have learned in the previous chapters, here is a list of do's and don'ts to follow when it comes to parenting stepchildren. You can use this as your guide to develop a good and loving relationship with your stepchildren.

DO defer to the biological parent

This does not mean that you have to be out of the picture. This only means that you should allow enough time for your relationship with your stepchildren to develop before you step in as a parent. You need to maintain your presence as a parent figure in the household by supporting the biological parent and by being there for the child. You should be the good cop and let your partner be the bad cop so that your stepchild will not develop any negative feelings toward you that will make it more difficult for you to form a close bond with him or her. If disciplinary action has to be taken, you should let your spouse do it. You should do the more fun or neutral roles, such as taking your stepchild to watch a sports game, bringing him or her to the dentist, buying school supplies with him or her, and so on.

DON'T set high expectations

Do not expect your stepchildren to love you the moment you meet each other or do not expect them to love you as much as their bio-parent right away. You should also avoid expecting the same interactions, bonds, communications, and feelings that you experienced with your biological children. Keep in mind that you were there from the time your biological children were born up to the present. You do not have the same shared history with your stepchildren. It is important to give the relationship time to develop naturally at its own pace.

DO allow your stepchildren to spend time with their biological parents

This may be difficult for you, but it is important to allow your stepchildren to spend time with their biological parents. You should not feel threatened as long as you are confident about your spouse's feelings. Allowing your stepchildren to spend time with their biological parents will give them the impression that you do not see it as a competition for your stepchildren's affection and that you want nothing more than to make your stepchildren happy.

DON'T show favorites

Do not always favor your biological children over your stepchildren because this will make your stepchildren despise you. Likewise, you should avoid overcompensating for your stepchildren just because you want them to accept and like you as their stepparent. This will only make things worse because the stepchildren will become used to it, which is not a good thing, and your biological children may harbor negative feelings toward you and their step siblings as well. Always show fairness, especially when it comes to discipline and allowances.

DO conduct regular family meetings

Family meetings give everyone a chance to express their thoughts and feelings about the current situation. This is the best time to share positive and negative comments and suggestions that will improve your relationships with one another and the family as a whole. Communicating regularly helps avoid misunderstandings and resolves conflicts right away before they become worse. You can do your meetings every weekend and make sure that each and every family member has a chance to speak while others are listening attentively.

DON'T overstep your boundaries

Do not make the mistake of overstepping your boundaries. For example, do not over discipline your stepchild or they will only end up hating you. You should allow you relationship to develop before you impose disciplinary actions on the kids. You should also step back when it comes to attending parent-teacher meetings at school because this is the job of the bio-parent. Anything that has something to do with the child's education should be handled by the bio-parents. You should also let the bio-parents help your stepchildren discuss major life decisions, like which high school or college to attend and what major to take. Unless your partner's ex is out of the picture, you should leave these things to your spouse and his or her ex.

DO discover your child's interests

Establishing a relationship with your stepchildren is pretty much the same as starting a new friendship. You need to discover what your stepchildren like that you can discuss or do together. For instance, if your stepchild likes to play the piano, you can talk about famous pianists with him/her, buy him/her a baby grand piano that they can play, or enroll them in piano lessons. You can also take them to a piano concert as a way for you to bond together. It is important to build a friendship with the child first before doing any form of parenting so that the relationship starts off on a positive note.

DON'T try too hard

Some stepparents come on too strong, which only irritates the child. Do not buy your stepchildren lots of gifts just to get on their good side or do not pretend to be a cool parent by liking everything that your stepchild likes because children will know that you are just trying to win their affection. Just be yourself and be real. Do not force yourself into your stepchildren's lives if they are not yet ready. Just let things develop naturally, and do not go against what you believe in just to make your stepchildren like you because this is not something that you want in your family.

DO find something right

You may think that your stepchildren hate you, but it is not true. They are just having a difficult time adjusting to the situation, and they end up taking out their anger, frustration, and confusion on you. You need to find something positive about your stepchildren that will keep you motivated to develop a good relationship with them instead of always complaining to your spouse about their negative attitude and behavior. You should also avoid complaining about your stepchildren all the time because this only puts your spouse in a difficult position where he/she feels like they have to choose between you and the kids. You are an adult, and you are one of the parents in the household, so be sure to act like one and handle things in a mature way instead of complaining all the time.

DON'T take things personally

As previously mentioned, your stepchildren do not really hate you. They just feel mad about the situation because they are being forced to adjust to changes that their parents caused. Given that you are part of those changes, it is natural that they see you in a negative light. You should not take it personally because this will only make it difficult for you to develop a good relationship with your stepchildren. Your stepchildren are already having a difficult time dealing with their parents' divorce and adjusting to a new home. Do not be an additional burden by being the evil stepparent. Be nice to your stepchildren because they have suffered enough.

These are the do's and don'ts of stepparenting that every stepparent needs to know. Some of them may not be easy to follow for everyone, but be sure to try your best because these tips have done wonders for a lot of blended families. You, as the stepparent, should be the one to reach out your hand to your stepchildren, and not the other way around, if you want to form a bond and establish a loving relationship with them.

Matthew Massimo and Sofia Price

Conclusion

Thank you again for downloading this book! I sincerely hope that you received value from it.

I hope this book was able to help you to understand the principles behind good stepparenting and how you can apply these concepts to your own family. I'm confident that if you apply what you have learned, you can achieve a long lasting and harmonious relationship with your stepchildren. The road toward a successful family may be difficult and may require a lot of work, but the rewards and joys you will gain are truly worth all the effort.

Finally, if you enjoyed this book, then I'd like to ask you for a favor, would you be kind enough to leave a review for this book on Amazon? Sofia and I want to reach as many people as we can with this book, and more reviews will help us accomplish that!

Thank you, and good luck!

Matthew Massimo and Sofia Price

BONUS Chapter – The 5 Biggest Mistakes Stepparents Make

Here are the five biggest mistakes that stepfamilies commonly make. These mistakes are presented in this book so you can avoid committing them.

Mistake #1: They do not have a blueprint for the success of their stepfamily.

Before building a house, we first need to create a blueprint to guide us during construction. The same is required for building a successful stepfamily. It is not enough that you take and use another stepfamily's blueprint and apply it to your own situation. Many stepparents unknowingly assume that their roles are the same as that of a biological mother or father – which really is not the case. They assume that the stepchildren will have the same enthusiasm about the success of the parent's marriage.

This is not completely true because the parents in the stepfamily are composed of one biological parent and one stepparent. It is wrong to assume that what makes you happy as a couple, such as wedding anniversaries and date nights, will also make your stepchildren happy, because the truth is that they don't, not really. Do not assume that the joys of your new stepfamily can completely erase the stepchildren's sadness caused by the loss of their old family.

Your success as a stepfamily will come by learning as much as you can about the new family that you will be creating, even prior to your marriage. Your success will also depend on how flexible you are in making changes to your plans as you learn more about one another. Be open to the questions and uncertainties that come with building a new stepfamily so you can find the right answers.

Mistake #2: They have no parenting plans.

Around 50 to 75 percent of dating couples with kids do not really discuss their plans for parenting prior to marriage. This is quite alarming because a lot of the stress and anxieties that you will experience when you become a stepparent pertain to step parenting, parenting, and even co-parenting the kids. You and your spouse need to know the restrictions that come with being a stepparent and how both of you can play to each other's strengths. You can become successful in creating harmony within your stepfamily when you understand how to create emotional attachment with your stepchildren, how their experiences affect them, and what you can do help them move on from their difficult past experiences.

Mistake #3: They expect too much, too soon.

One of the negative consequences of mistake #1 is that you will have the wrong expectation that just because you and your spouse are happy, your stepchildren will quickly be happy, too. When you see that this is not happening, both you and your spouse can start to become confused and frustrated. You will start questioning yourself: "What am I doing wrong?" or "Maybe it is wrong to marry a previously married man/woman." With the first statement, you are casting blame on yourself, which is wrong; with the second statement, you are starting to unravel your commitment to your marriage.

To avoid becoming frustrated, you need to know that it normally takes several years to build harmony within your new stepfamily. Remember that it just cannot happen quickly. You will only make it worse when you always second-guess yourself and you blame either yourself or other people. You need to consistently remind yourself to be more determined and to persevere until you find all the answers you are looking for in building a successful stepfamily.

Mistake #4: Forcing blendering.

The term "blendering" pertains to what married couples do to compel their family members to blend in together. It is a wrong assumption when it comes to building a successful stepfamily. You cannot really simply put in all the ingredients (the members of your new stepfamily) into a blender and use intense force until they are mixed or blended together. Blendering is ideal if you want to make a smoothie, but it is ineffective when it comes to dealing with your stepchildren. With blendering, you expect that affection and deep love between you and your stepchildren to come quickly, and then you set out to make it happen in your own time frame.

You need to realize that when it comes to your stepfamily's success, you need to use the "crockpot" instead of the "blender." You need to allow each of the ingredients to relax and combine at a very slow pace. As a stepparent, you need to create lasting relationships with your stepchildren, but do not place high expectations on yourself and on the kids. You need to continually engage your stepchildren over time until you are able to create a deep connection with them through love and trust.

Mistake #5: They do not manage fear.

Even though you and your spouse may be filled with joy and hope because of your new marriage, you really cannot deny that you still feel afraid sometimes because you worry whether your marriage will be successful or will only lead to another divorce. If you have experienced divorce, the hurt that it brought to your life can cause you to fear that it might happen again.

If you do not manage these fears properly, you and your spouse will end up being hesitant, easily cautious, and untrusting. These negativities can erode your marriage regardless of how committed you are to each other at the start. You need to be open to your spouse about your fears so you can discuss issues and appease each other. You need to declare your love and commitment to each other continuously so that your marriage, which is the foundation of your stepfamily, will remain strong and secure.